This book belongs to:

Blitz's Perfect Day

Stella Rain

Identifiers:
LCCN: 2023936202
ISBN: (paperback) 979-8-9876337-4-8
ISBN: (hardcover) 979-8-9876337-5-5
ISBN: (ebook) 979-8-9876337-6-2
Available in paperback, hardback, and e-book

Illustrations by Stella Rain
Layout by Felicity Fox Books Publishing House

Published by Felicity Fox Books Publishing House
Kissimmee, FL 34747
www.thefelicityfoxhouse.com

Blitz's Perfect Day

Stella Rain

Felicity Fox Books Publishing House

Hi! My name is Blitz.

I'm a lucky dog because I live with a loving human.

My fur is black and gold and super soft.

I love to run and play outside!

My favorite place is by the pond.

I walk around the pond and look for frogs.

A frog jumps into the water.

So, I jump into the water and swim across the pond to see a turtle.

And then the turtle jumps into the water too!

Then, I stand very still on the dock and watch the fish in the water.

For a very long time I stand there, watching and listening closely.

My human is always by the pond with me.

When I'm done with my adventures, my human calls me inside.

"Come here, Blitz! Time to come in!"

My human dries me with a soft towel.

My human lets me inside after my fur is dry.

I lay down on my bed.

Once I close my eyes, I take a nap.

My dreams take me back to my adventures at the pond.

I am a lucky dog!

About the Author

Stella was born and raised in a small quaint town in NY. As a child, she enjoyed stomping in the puddles after a rainstorm, playing in the creek, various outings, and getting together with family and friends. She has two children. In her free time, she gardens and harvests plants, spends time with her grandson, and spends a lot of time with Blitz.

About Blitz

Blitz may be his formal name, but his human calls him Blitzy Blue, and some friends call him Zippy or Bedazzle. Blitz is an energetic, smart, beautiful dog who was rescued from the pound. Blitz craved room to run and explore and he got exactly that with his human! He is very happy and enjoys all aspects of the outdoors and his rides in the buggy. He also loves to visit with his many friends.

Upcoming Projects

Stella hopes you enjoy the fun, colorful pages of Blitz's adventures!

For more about the wonderful world of Blitz, upcoming books, and free coloring pages, visit Stella's website at ...